Helpful Tips For Any Type of Business

Part II- The expanded Edition

Authored by Christi Hubbard

Patriotic & Family Oriented Business owner CFC 19270

ISBN-13: 978-1500478698

ISBN-10: 1500478695

Dedication:

I need to give thanks to my Mom, Janet Hubbard Shreve for always believing in me. Also to God above for always guiding me true and straight.

I give thanks to my wonderful and steadfast friends and business associates who always give wonderful suggestions. "You know so much you should be a consultant and charge for your knowledge." "You should write a book."

I give thanks to my sons, Matthew and Mark Myers for helping me out with my company clients while I took the time to jump right in and write the book inside a month.

Thank you to Melissa Vazquez, an author in her own right, for sharing CreateSpace with me so I could easily write and self-publish the book.

I have expressed my own opinions and business reviews based on my experience with these companies and people referred to in the book. I encourage you to do your homework when you first start your own business, partner, collaborate, or do anything legally binding.

Table of Contents:

Introduction

A little background. I own and operate three companies all with one goal in mind, to help others in need. I will be writing about my personal and professional experiences while still keeping my clients confidential. If by educating and speaking about what I've encountered helps just one person, it will be worth it.

Animal Rescue & Veteran Support Services, Corp (Veteran Rescue ®) is a 501c3 nonprofit created by Ms. Christi Hubbard (primary owner, founder and CFO) to use animal assisted therapy to assist Veterans in their rehabilitation and reorientation through various services. Since 2011 we have been assisting veterans with home repair projects, rehabilitating rescued animals and paring them together to heal both with plenty of care. http://veteranrescue.org **We have won 2 awards to date. Veteran Rescue ® is a registered trademark of Animal Rescue & Veteran Support Services, Corp. christi@veteranrescue.org** **"A Warrior's Sanctuary"**

100% tax deductible receipts. #VeteranRescue #taxdeductible #animalshelter #dog #cat #donate #veteran #PTSD #retreat #horse #therapy

Wildcat's Sanctuary and Ranch Corp is called upon to handle all kinds of questions, pets, and furry children. You can see them as we walk them, play with them, introduce them to others, and in some cases steer clear of them so mom doesn't abandon them.

Summer means pet sitters are in high demand. Schedule your sitter today and know peace of mind. christi@wildcatsanctuaryranch.com

We have won 4 awards to date.
http://www.wildcatsanctuaryranch.com/

We are experienced in all manner of breeds and are licensed and insured. We have been voted the best in Lake Mary 4 years in a row. We support humane handling of our animals, using lots of love and treats and no, harsh choker collars, shock collars, or expensive courses. Our work is done right in our home and neighborhood. We offer multiple discounts and accept credit card payments. "Ask for the Best, Ask for Wildcat!"

#Wildcat #Sanctuary #Ranch #AskForTheBest #PetSitter

#Dog #cat #animals #bunny #bird #LakeMary #awardWinning

Welcome to Home For Heroes ®

Home For Heroes ® Ms. Christi Hubbard (primary owner) uses PTSD videos and Reality TV in showcasing Veterans healing on the ranch. A percentage of all proceeds are donated to Veteran Rescue ®.

Home For Heroes ® is a registered trademark of Home For Heroes Productions, LLC. "United We Stand, Divided We Fail."

To contact for more information, interest in investing or being filmed please email info@homeforheroestv.com
http://www.homeforheroestv.com/

Amazon smile. Thank you for shopping!
http://smile.amazon.com/ch/32-0337515

I was raised on a small ten acre farm in the woods of Brooksville, Florida, with lots of animals, where I actively cared for a variety of pets since I was a small child. These early experiences had a profound impact on me. Later, I noticed a distinct lack of animal care in my area when owners traveled on vacation. The owners often boarded their pets with a vet, typically in cages. Wildcat (My love of animals is partially the reason I earned the moniker "Wildcat". I also showed the tenacity of a wild cat in my fighting techniques during my police academy training, so "Wildcat" was a natural fit.) asked, "Who wants to stay in a cage all day?" The answer – No one!

I have handled horses, rabbits, ferrets, cats, dogs, birds, hamsters and gerbils. Years ago, I discovered an ability to catch and hold any animal whether feral or domestic, regardless of bites and claws. I also hand raised animal babies that were abandoned, sick or just taken too soon from their mother to ensure their health and well-being. My love of animals is partially the reason I earned the moniker "Wildcat". I also showed the tenacity of a wild cat in my fighting techniques during my police academy training, so "Wildcat" was a natural fit.

Throughout my adult life, I have gained a lot of different understanding through a lot of diverse work experiences. I have worked in Law Enforcement, and have two associate's degrees, one in Law Enforcement and the other in Criminology. I have earned multiple certificates and gathered a long line of military connections, which include my dad, a Marine, my nephew in the Air Force, a cousin and brother in law both in the Army. A father in law also retired from the Navy. I worked for three years for the local Sheriff's office. For fifteen years, I have worked as a receptionist, then two years as a teller. After that, I spent five years in security. I have also done house and pet sitting and volunteering.

#ChristiHubbard #Wildcat

Getting started: Which Is Right For You

For Profit: INC, Corp, LLC or Non Profit/Not For Profit 501c3

Costs Involved of each as of this writing: Varies By State

For Instance Florida: Provided By Sunbiz.org

Corporation Fees

PROFIT AND NON-PROFIT

Filing Fees $ 35.00

Registered Agent Designation $ 35.00

*Certified Copy (optional) $ 8.75

TOTAL $ 78.75

Limited Liability Company Fees

Annual Report (& Supplemental Fee) $ 138.75

Colorado Courtesy Of:
http://www.sos.state.co.us/pubs/info_center/fees/business.html

Profit corporations	Online fee	Paper fee
Articles of Incorporation	$50.00	n/a

Nonprofit corporations	Online fee	Paper fee
Articles of Incorporation	$50.00	n/a

Limited liability company	Online fee	Paper fee
Articles of Organization	$50.00	n/a

Kentucky Courtesy Of: http://www.sos.ky.gov/bus/business-filings/Pages/Fees.aspx

Domestic Corporations (Profit and Professional Service)

Articles of Incorporation: $40.00 (pursuant to KRS 136.060, profit entities must add organization tax based on number of shares)

Domestic Corporations (Non-Profit)

Articles of Incorporation: $8.00

Domestic Limited Liability Company (Profit, Non-Profit or Professional Service)

Articles of Organization: $40.00

Virginia Courtesy Of: http://www.scc.virginia.gov/clk/formfee.aspx

Virginia Stock Corporations

The number of the form relates to the applicable statute in Title 13.1 of the Code of Virginia. All fee payments should be made payable to the State Corporation Commission.

SCC FORM #/FORMAT   FORM TITLE   FILING FEE/COMMENTS

Notice-DOC

Notice-PDF

Notice to Virginia Corporations

Charter/Entrance-DOC

Charter/Entrance-PDF

Corporation Charter/Entrance Fee Schedule

Washington DC Courtesy Of:
http://dcra.dc.gov/service/register-domestic-entity

General Corporate Filing - All Entities

Corporations Division Fees - General Corporate Filing - All Entities

Entity Type	Fee Description	Fee Amount
All Domestic & Foreign Filing Entities	Expedited same-day service	$100.00
All Domestic & Foreign Filing Entities	Expedited three day service	$50.00

Division Fees - Nonprofit Corporation

Corporations Division Fees - Nonprofit Corporation

Entity Type	Fee Description	Fee Amount
Domestic Nonprofit Corporation	Articles of incorporation	$80.00

Corporations Division Fees - Limited Liability Company

Corporations Division Fees - Limited Liability Company

Entity Type	Fee Description	Fee Amount
Domestic Limited Liability Company	Certificate of organization	$220.00

Washington Courtesy Of:
https://www.sos.wa.gov/corps/FEESCHEDULEEXPEDITEDSERVICE.aspx

Limited Liability Companies (Title 25.15 RCW)

Original Filings	$180

Profit Corporations (Title 23B RCW)

Original Filings $180

Non-profit Corporations (Title 24.03 RCW)

Original Filings $ 30

Limited Liability Partnerships (Title 25.05 RCW)

Application for Registration $180

Texas Courtesy Of: https://direct.sos.state.tx.us/help/help-corp.asp?pg=fee

Information Requests, Copies & Certificates   Fee

Certificate of Fact (including Certificate of Existence or Status) $15

Long Form Certificate of Existence (Status plus list of filings) $25

As you can see pricing varies widely based on location and type of company being created.

Next up: If you choose Non-profit, IRS 501c3 application which is called Form 1023. http://www.irs.gov/pub/irs-pdf/f1023.pdf This is free to file, even expedited which is what every non-profit should ask for.

Also if in Florida and additional form must be obtained to allow you to solicit for donations at http://www.freshfromflorida.com/Business-Services/Search-by-Business/Charitable-Organizations

Non-Profits also are required to obtain General Liability insurance (roughly $600/Year in Florida) and D&O Insurance (Director and Officers for Board Members again roughly

$600/year in Florida. Each state and insurance company quotes vary widely.

All Businesses except Pet Sitting, which is an unregulated industry, are required to obtain State Registration, Licensing, and carry insurance; General Liability Insurance policies of at least $1,000,000 or more. Your city Tax Collector's Office is where you obtain a license to operate a business in certain counties, Florida, Seminole County is currently $10/year.

You also have to have a tax account; in Florida it's http://dor.myflorida.com/dor/taxes/sales_tax.html .You also request tax exempt status here: http://dor.myflorida.com/dor/forms/current/dr5.pdf

It does not matter what industry you start a business in or even if you are an author writing books, this information pertains to just about every one of us entrepreneurs.

Get involved in groups; Chamber of Commerce meetings, introduce yourself to influential people in your county, city and state.

If you are a shy introvert, partner up with or get a volunteer that's passionate about your cause that is an outgoing extrovert.

PASSION is the KEY to being asked to do interviews. It is also the key to obtaining volunteers for your Board and company events.

What are the main differences between a Corporation, Not For Profit AKA Non-Profit and an LLC?

Corporation (Corp) Has shares of stock you can sell privately to known friends, family and associates or wait until your company is doing really well and get on the NYSE Market with your shares of stock and sell to everyone.

LLC (Limited Liability Corporation) has no shares of stock but when someone sues you they can't go after your personal property.

501c3, Not for Profit, Non-Profit- Charitable, 100% Tax Deductible, Tax Exempt from sales tax, can hold fundraisers and solicit for funds.

Next step in this process? Putting all the forms and documents you need together and knowing where or how to get them registered. I am always available to help others regardless of their location. I also don't charge an arm and a leg to help you either.

Partnerships, Collaborations and Promises

As a business owner you always look to enriching and opening up your network to utilize collaborations or partners. In doing so you are looking at that person's track record, reputation, services offered, and how they sync with your own before making the initial approach.

I have made some bad collaboration choices and some good ones. I will tell you what mistakes I made and how to avoid them.

Bad choice #1: Take someone's word as gospel truth just because they say they are a military Veteran.

How to avoid this: Check around. See what connections you have in common and ask for referral or how long they've known. Check to see if they are a Veteran. They should be able to provide you with a copy of DD-214, if not you can check via a person you know is a Veteran, as they have access to resources a civilian does not. Google them; what are others saying about them?

Bad Choice #2: Collaborative Partnership: Get all legal documents signed first. I actually have documents still outstanding to be signed and returned from legit Veteran owned companies we have recently collaborated with. We actually had our business name stolen by someone in Oregon. FAR put that stolen and fraudulent info on our SAM record. (This what government contractors use when they are looking to sign a contract for millions of dollars usually for the government which is renewed every two or three years. It is a very lucrative deal if your company passes all the inspections of documents, so having fraudulent information is a big no no and can actually have your company black balled from ever being allowed to compete for the contracts.)

How to avoid this: Be a pest. Get those documents signed. Be apologetic but sincere, and don't communicate further with details they need until those papers are signed.

Bad Choice #3: Services offered: Look to see that the service offered meshes with yours. Sometimes they may have a service you need and offer a good deal, you accept only to find out their promises are no good. Communication goes out the door.

How to avoid this: Find a company with a brick and mortar building, go to them, get everything in writing. I can't emphasize the importance of this enough. We all want to help our local startups. We all want to support our Veteran entrepreneurs. We don't want to be taken advantage of.

Experience we will always tell the tale. Do your homework, get collaborative partnership details written down into an MOU (Memorandum of Understanding, means a collaboration agreement which is a little different from a partnership agreement or merging of companies into one.) legally binding or an attorney to write up a true partnership document spelling out everything. Have confidential agreements ready to be signed. Get referrals and research done well before agreeing to anything. If you have a Board of Directors, get them involved. It's a part of their job to help you weed out questionable relationships. Always verify what you were told. In the end you'll be glad you did.

K.I.S.S. Method

I first learned about the K.I.S.S. Method (Keep It Simple Stupid) while attending the police academy. I have discovered this is what agencies want in their reports, whether that agency is police, security, bank, etc. Giving too much information does not help them make informed decisions.

When this method should not be utilized is when you are involved in fundraising, building collaboration MOU documents, partnership mergers, last will and testament, staff instructions, etc. Although staff instructions should have details it should be precise not K.I.S.S.

Fundraising Tips

The trick to a successful campaign is for everyone to share it, not just one person. Everyone who shares it, also likes it, and invites people to it if it's an event. Explain all the details so there's very little to question, give it to them in plenty of time and share, share, share. You don't know how often your post is being seen by others. I also have a list of organizations that nonprofits should utilize to really get their feet operational without breaking the budget.

If your organization has a 501c3 letter, please create your accounts: IT'S FREE!

Here are some logins we have for places you can get software, donations really cheap or even free. I'll leave off government logins as you probably won't be going after government contracts. If you decide you do want that, I can walk you through SAM, Cage, DUNS, and NAICS. We (as women) can also team up on government contracts as there are certain set asides held specifically for women owned businesses and are over $1 million a year.

SBA offers 8a certifications which open up a lot of state and federal donations of supplies. ~~FYI.~~
https://eweb.sba.gov/gls/dsp_login.cfm?CFID=10958620&CFTOKEN=3ae26b3d44984541-9955A6C7-CF5E-0B66-696D026F2B0511BF&jsessionid=5e30caf362087ed5537f7f3052412548164f

We have Grantstation for a year we received for $99. via Techsoup, which lists every-foundation, individual, and others who give grant money to 501c3 nonprofits.
http://grantstation.com/

http://techsoup.org/ is an excellent resource for software. For instance, we have Office 2013 suite for just $30. We received QuickBooks there too, again very cheap and affordable for those on a shoestring budget.

CFC (combined Federation Campaign) is the biggest source of funding per year. Again, it takes a 501c3 certification. One county in Florida donated $10,000.00 to us this year. Next year we already have four states approved. It also went Universal, which means if someone has our CFC number, 19270, then they can donate no matter what state they are in and it automatically goes into our Nonprofit account. The downside here is the funds are paid quarterly, monthly, or one time payment depending on area and how much money was donated to your charity and fees apply. I'm told big changes are coming for FY 2014 which is going Universal and more fees apply.

Good360 http://good360.com/

Guidestar.org rates nonprofits and accepts donations for them.

Amazon Smile: http://smile.amazon.com/

Only 1 Agency wants specialized 501c3 to apply with state licensing to back them or SBA 8A certification.

Fleet and Federal Surplus Property.

Also special note: the US Government holds auctions where you bid on pallets of items you need. This is a useful way to obtain start up needs.

MOU Agreements and Partner Mergers of companies should be very detailed as they are a legal document. You want to let the other organization or company know exactly where each party stands in relation to starting out, active executive directives, operational line of command, in case things don't work out.

Last will and testament should be precise because you want people to know you have one and you want them to obey it. It's your life and death we're talking about here, So be clear. K.I.S.S. While detailed is the way to go-you don't want to confuse the executor.

You would think by giving more information you would be imparting more data for the person to make an informed decision, in reality you just confused the poor person.

#fundraising #notforprofits #nonprofits #taxdeductible #MOU

Service Dog or Pet

How to tell the difference between a Service Dog and a Pet with a Vest. Keep in mind there is also a Therapy Pet. So to classify in order of health related benefits and training:

Service Dog: The most strenuous training. Final test is videotaped. Most Service Dogs are raised from a litter that had specific breeding criteria. Some are rescued and then trained. Vest or ID indicating a Service Dog is not required by law but will immediately them as one. If a person has a Service Dog, by law you cannot ask what is wrong with them or why they need one. You cannot deny them entrance anywhere. A Service Dog performs a specific task required to help the person who is the handler. The pair train together.

Therapy Dog/Pet: Therapy Pets I say pets because any pet can provide therapy services but not be fully trained. These dogs may have training but for one reason or another does not qualify for Service Also, they go anywhere with the person-and they cannot wear a vest that says Service Dog or Service in Training.

Pet: Obedience trained but when out in public displays aggression, bad behavior and does not immediately obey commands.

Always check to make sure you are dealing with a reputable agency or organization when it comes to picking a dog.

You may have heard these complaints: "Get tired of seeing individuals claim a service pet that has a vest but fits in a handbag or a small carrier. Seeing them come into a grocery store or a restaurant, or church! Bit much and seems that many do it for attention. How can a dog the size of a rat when it is wet be called a service animal?"

There are widely debated pros/cons of any type of dog being used for a Service Dog. What is important is the bond created, the training, and passing of a videotaped test proving the dog in question can perform the needed services and functions for the human.

We approve of http://www.k9sforwarriors.org/ They do an excellent job with training real Service dogs, just like http://www.guidedogs.org/ .

Working with Animals

I have been working with animals since childhood. Each represents its own unique challenges.

Horses: Bite, kick, rear, have colic, go riding, buck you off

Dogs: ~~Feral or tame~~: bite, scratch deep grooves, run away, poop/pee in house, may be aggressive or beta

Cats: Feral or tame: bite, scratch deep grooves, run away, poop/pee in house, aggressive or beta

Bunnies: They kick, scratch and bite when hopping mad. It takes a lot to get them that way though.

Birds: Large, small, talking

Fish: Fresh or salt water

Reptiles: Snakes, Iguanas

Cows: These guys will generally leave you alone. Bulls will not.

Goats: Easy to maintain. They will eat anything.

Let's start by discussing potty training. Recently I've been helping train a 6 month old rescue/bought from store. The owner uses unscented puppy potty pads. ~~unscented~~. I recommend Nature's Miracle products because they are all natural, eat the pheromones and enzymes leaving house and furniture smelling like furniture and not an outhouse. These products don't harm the pets or the humans. Right now we are using bleach cleaner.

Kennel training vs Potty pads vs notice pick up and deposit outside while going to train:

I have used two out of three. When puppies are born I begin training when they start walking. See them start to pee or poop? Pick them up and immediately place them outside where you want them to go. Repeat often.

Kennel training is when you place the dog inside a crate for sleeping then take outside immediately you open it in the morning. Some people leave dogs in kennels all day long. Not me. When potty training, they should sleep in there at night and in the morning go outside. Then you bring back them inside and watch carefully until you're sure there will be no accidents.

Potty pads is where you place them on the floor you want the dog to go on then slowly reduce area size covered and move closer to the door until the dog is going outside only. Some puppy pads are scented with pheromones to encourage dogs to only go on that pad.

Training is key no matter the animals. You get what you put into it. (I would strongly stress here the time involved in successfully housetraining an animal. You have to devote a good week of 24/7!) Be knowledgeable about who you hire if not doing it yourself. Make sure they're not being abused or neglected in the name of training. I suggest you ask tons of questions from different reputable people, read books, articles to keep on top of all the changes.

It takes a special kind of person to be able to handle feral animals correctly-then socialize them into pets. I am one of those people. It is quite often painful in the beginning as no matter your care you will be bitten, clawed up and chase the animal around and around until cornered. It usually takes a team of three or more people to care for one animal when trying to get it in the travel kennel for a vet visit or for applying flea medicine or for giving a bath. First experiences color the pet's view for life, handle with care!

Welcome to
VETERAN RESCUE

www.veteranrescue.org
Veteran Rescue ® is a registered trademark of Animal Rescue & Veteran Support Services, Corp.

Equine Therapy

Therapy doesn't have to be intimidating. Through recreational therapy, Veterans can achieve greatness together with animal and human companions. Veteran Rescue offers the following:

Benefits

Can grooming and riding horses foster recovery from mental illness? According to a recent article published in the Psychiatric Times, the answer is "Yes." "Evidence has continued to accumulate; more rigorous controlled studies are being conducted, resulting in the emergence of a significant body of literature supporting the therapeutic value of the human-companion animal interaction." An article reviewing the benefits of animal-assisted therapy has even appeared in the prestigious Journal of the American Medical Association.
http://ps.psychiatryonline.org/article.aspx?articleid=81469 and https://www.avma.org/KB/Policies/Pages/Guidelines-for-Animal-Assisted-Activity-Animal-Assisted-Therapy-and-Resident-Animal-Programs.aspx

Benefits of Equine Therapy

Animal-assisted therapy has shown evidenced-based efficacy in patients including war veterans with PTSD, depression, anxiety, attention-deficit/hyperactivity disorder, conduct disorders, dissociate disorders, and other chronic mental illnesses. In light of research and observational findings, experts suggest that Equine Therapy a common form of animal-assisted therapy–may yield a variety of psychotherapeutic benefits.

What we will accomplish:

- Confidence
- Self-efficacy
- Self-concept
- Communication
- Trust
- Perspective
- Anxiety reduction
- Decreasing isolation
- Self-acceptance
- And much more.

PTSD Treatment Options

Not every treatment is offered at your VA Hospital or clinic.

- Cognitive Behavioral Treatments for PTSD these include: Exposure Therapy, Stress-Inoculation Training, and Cognitive Processing Therapy.
- Psychodynamic Psychotherapy for PTSD
- Acceptance and Commitment Therapy
- Medications for PTSD
- Treatments for the Co-Occurrence of PTSD and Substance Use
- PTSD and Hypnosis
- PTSD and Depression go hand in hand with mTBI and TBI
- Evidence based treatment
- Recreational based treatment
- Equine Therapy

Know Your Worth!

I just had to talk about this. I know several of my friends can attest to this as well.

A recent conversation: "Your prices are too high!" My vet only charges $20/day to board in the cages", I want $10/day for your services." I charge $40/day to have run of the home, frequent playtime and walks through nature's harvest.

I go to my competitors and look at their prices. Let's compare:

Large dog: $25/day for 6 by 8 room, playtime extra, 4 or 5 vaccination shots required, extra walks, extra money.

Large Dog: $50/day, 4 or 5 vaccination shots required, everything extra, holidays double priced!

Vets offices cages only, $20-60/day, no extras

Me: Run of the home, only Rabies is required by law so that is all I ask for, playtime all day, no charge! Extra walks, no charge! As in this particular case once an hour; sometimes three times an hour as dog is old and has cancer. Home has Oriental carpets and regular carpets to go with tile and wood floors. Cleaning costs for floors is included in my prices.

Results: I had already guaranteed a deep discount of $20/day. I stood by that, yet I did not get that client's business. That is okay. I know my worth. This was a one-time exception. It will not happen again. I give discounts to Military and long term clients.

Know your worth. I don't take every potential client that comes my way looking for rock bottom prices or even less than going rates. I have won 4 consecutive awards for my quality of service.

To learn more: http://www.wildcatsanctuaryranch.com/

I also keep my recommendations on my website. I have multiple client referrals. You can research me on Google reviews, LinkedIn, and on my website, and let's not forget Facebook. I'm looking at joining Angie's List next.

The reason I tell you this is because if you sacrifice your worth for one person, next thing you know here comes a referral: "Well you did it for them, do it for me." Your services are costing you time, money, chemicals, employees, insurance, gas, vehicle repair and much more. Research your competitors and know your worth. The lowest fees on the block do not guarantee you clients. It may in fact guarantee you get none! I have spoken to many other business owners and this is a frequent complaint. If this has happened with you and you want to share how you handled it, please comment!.

Programs

Recently we have been reevaluating the Programs we offer: Should we add more, remove some, put spending caps on them, documentation we ask for, etc.

It was brought home to me quite recently that I can't help everyone and that ~~by~~ trying to please everyone only drains my limited resources that much quicker.

I have a very unique niche and I should stick to it.

Based on the kinds of requests for help we've been receiving, it was decided a reasonable cap help us keep our budget under control.

The kinds of documentation we ask for and receive in order to assist a client is reasonable, legal, and necessary in case of audits. Any nonprofit should expect to be audited frequently as they grow bigger and handle more and more funds.

As for the programs we offer we are evaluating the Home Repair Project and decided not to add anything more to what we already offer, regardless of whether it's a good fit for my Mission and Vision.

I can't stress enough the importance of documenting everything, even with people on your Advisory Board. Document every conversation, and suggestion made in case of future malfeasance, which we've already weathered a few times.

People think that because I am woman owned business helping Veterans and animals it is okay to lie to me, try to use me for their own gain, agree to handshake deals only and more. However, I have honor, integrity, faith, and I keep my dealings above board and transparent. I always answer any question asked of me in regards to my business. If something is confidential it stays that way.

Confidentiality of Businesses You Interact With

I am going to talk about what I know, how I did it and tips you can use. You can ask me questions, submit comments or suggestions. It's all about educating others so they don't make the same mistakes I did. We are all going to make them regardless. My mistakes cost me money and inventory. Every time you start a business you are building your reputation. Every person you interact with will either hinder you or help you. My goal is to help others. This forum helps us reach others outside our network which in the end helps us out.

In this book I actually do name names in the context of whether this business provides quality or can you find something better. We replaced names with *"Removed for privacy."* This is usually because in that instance the person or company was blameless. We learned from Chris Kyle's book and his widow being sued over something in the book. So we made sure to include all facts in the book from both sides.

Privacy is all well and good but sometimes the greater good comes from exposing those you really should avoid. Accountability means Transparency. And if certain people refused to sign non disclaimers then they can't complain when it comes back to bite them.

Budgeting: Getting It Right the First Time

I actually had help from an existing company putting my budget together. I have a very detailed Excel formatted budget that goes from startup costs, to monthly recurring costs, to annual recurring costs. I then asked various ranch owners in different states about the costs of running their ranches. They were very open. Now, Budgets for Government Contracts are a whole different sort of numbers. Think in the millions and paid out quarterly with audits to continue with your contract or set aside. Then there are the Budgets for Grant Applications for your 501c3 nonprofit. I have them all. I have included them just so you see the huge difference it makes.

The Good, The Bad, The Ugly in the Corporate World of Products

Through my experience I have listed places for signs and brochures or business cards being printed up for you.

VistaPrint produces so so quality at cheap prices. http://FRSigns.com however produces top notch quality at best prices I've found.

Trademark Press works with you, but they had a complete file loss so every time I needed to re-order I had to find old files to re-submit and disputes in invoice pricing, amount paid were often ignored. It was their final say so we stopped using them after paying them off. Our nonprofit money needs accountability and Trademark Press did not offer that.

I have used all 3 companies named. It is only my opinions stated. I encourage you to find your own budget friendly printer.

What companies have I found that are outstanding and would recommend to anyone? Very FEW and here they are:

Jack Pagano: jackp1957@gmail.com

For almost six years Jack has been in the Afghanistan fight-training, mentoring and advising in all facets of Broadcasting and Strategic Communications. He worked with President Karzai's office, the US Embassy in Afghanistan and for Gen John Allen at ISAF. While at ISAF he produced "Game Changing" video overviews and strategic communications work concerning Security Force Assistance (SFA) and Insider Threat (IT) solutions. This work is saving lives everyday.

He was also a key member in building and developing Afghanistan's Government Media and Information Center (GMIC) in its vital mission to prepare a generation of Afghan media managers with the skills needed to deliver messages of peace and stability in the war torn country of Afghanistan. He has trained more than three hundred Afghans in the art of communications. Jack has three plus decades of civilian, military and documentary broadcasting experience. He has produced powerful video work for Former Secretary of State GEN Colin Powell, Oliver North and President's Bush and Clinton.

Jack is a retired Army Lieutenant Colonel with extensive hands-on overseas, called back to active duty experience in: Desert Storm, Bosnia, Kosovo and Operation Iraqi Freedom. Jack's commercial broadcasting experience includes stints as a Pentagon Correspondent and Producer for FOX News, Executive Producer at FOX Dallas, Texas, and Prepro Producer/Supervisor at WSVN Miami, Florida. In 2005, Jack was a coordinating producer and videographer for Nick and Jessica Simpson's 2-hour ABC TV special, "TOUR OF DUTY." During that special Jack shot and edited a music video that aired worldwide. And in 2006, Jack shot, edited, and produced with two Iraqi advisors a dynamic music video, "Baghdad My Love" a number one music video for almost a year. The music video was part of the successful GEN David Petraeus "Surge" initiative.

Jack's broadcasting career began as an NBC Page in New York. He continues to seek out work that will inspire, educate, and empower audiences everywhere. Jack Pagano is an award-winning producer who creates impassioned productions.

"…No one wants peace more than a soldier, but no one wants to be tested more than a soldier…"

Circle of Seven Productions: Sheila Clover English

http://cosproductions.com/

A video production and marketing company specializing in the publishing industry. Featured in The New York Times and The Wall Street Journal Circle of Seven Productions is the first book video production company and trademarked the term "book trailer".

From video to video distribution and social media marketing, we work with large publishers, small publishers and authors offering affordable packages and award winning creative.

Specialties

Book Video, Award Winning Creative, Social Media Marketing, Online and Offline Advertising

Fairway Recognition Signs: http://www.frsigns.com/ **888-661-0166**

Tournament signs, banners of any kinds, brochures, flyers, and more. Best deals and excellent quality!! For example 18 signs were $300. 1 3 ft by 8 ft banner was $182. Full color spectrum, as many colors as you have.

Trustco Bank: http://www.trustcobank.com/

Trustco works with very small businesses, miniscule budgets, as well as large companies and personal accounts too. They are very helpful and do all they can for their clients.

Superior Lawn Care: Charles 407-492-7300
http://www.superiorlawncareinc.com/ **: Awesome service.**

Kenny and his team always look out for your yard. They will tell you what you need to spray for if a critter pops up that destroys your lawn and Superior isn't providing your pesticides. They do offer. He will trim back shrubs that are breaking and blocking your sprinklers. He listens attentively, very polite too. Also he will have everyone stop if you come outside or drive up so you're not covered in grass and blowing trim.

We have had 4 different lawn care services they ended up causing hundreds of dollars in damage. We pay more but have excellent service and NO DAMAGE!

Computer Techs Castle: http://computertechscastle.com/

Computer Techs Castle Repairs / Contracts

Computer Techs Castle, LLC is a computer company in Lake Mary, Florida, that serves individuals and businesses. The following is from their business literature:

We specialize in computer, server, and VoIP installations, though we also offer custom Ethernet cabling and computer repairs. In addition, we have Security Specialists that can provide all encompassing computer security and internet security services. With more than 15 years of experience, we provide quality service in order to exceed your expectations. Our customers choose us because of our affordable prices and top-of-the-line equipment.

Here at Computer Techs Castle, no matter what condition your computer is in we can repair it back to good as new. Our customers receive great customer service. We install Servers, Desktops, Laptops, We provide services for Network+, A+ hardware, server security, Network security, security specialists, We repair Desktops, Laptops, Servers

We appreciate you taking the time to review us and take a look at what we offer. If you have any questions or concerns feel free to give us a call or email.

Have a wonderful blessed day!   Certified & Insured

THL: The Hallow Life: MMORPG:
http://www.thehallowlife.com/forums/

The Hallow Life - An MMORPG in development! Featuring very real life like simulations and has concepts no other game does.

Halogix Technologies:

Matthew is a programmer and designer of games through his company. He has been interested in computers since he was young, teaching himself hardware and programming. Matthew understands numerous programming languages for website design and for game design and is a valuable security specialist as well as a programmer and web designer.

Veteran Rescue Annual Expense Report

50 Acres, 25 Employees, 6 Horses

EXPENSE CATEGORY	Expenses - Variable		Expenses - Fixed		Start Up Costs	Breakeven	
	Monthly	Annual	Monthly	Annual		Monthly	Annual
Gas Utilities	$ 200.00	$ 2,400.00					
Electric	$ 1,000.00	$ 12,000.00					
Mortgage			$ 1,250.00	$ 15,000.00			
Phone			$ 100.00	$ 1,200.00			
Cable			$ 100.00	$ 1,200.00			
Internet			$ 100.00	$ 1,200.00			
Entertainment Food	$ 1,250.00	$ 15,000.00					
Marketing/Advertising	$ 1,750.00	$ 21,000.00					
Funding Manager			$ 12,000.00	$ 144,000.00			
Cleaning Supplies	$ 250.00	$ 3,000.00					
Vitamins	$ 150.00	$ 1,300.00					
Purchase land					$ 150,000.00		
Construct buildings					$ 150,000.00		
Repair Premises					$ 50,000.00		
Fence in Land					$ 25,000.00		
Purchase Equipment					$ 200,000.00		
Purchase Electronics					$ 50,000.00		
Purchase Office Supplies					$ 10,000.00		
Gas for company vehicles	$ 400.00	$ 4,800.00					
Purchase Horses					$ 5,000.00		
Purchase Dogs					$ 5,000.00		
Purchase other animals					$ 5,000.00		
Pet supplies, horse feed/hay	$ 2,500.00	$ 30,000.00					
Purchase company vehicles					$ 30,000.00		
Veterinarian Services	$ 2,500.00	$ 30,000.00					
Medical	$ 2,500.00	$ 30,000.00					
Insurances				$ 10,000.00			
Property Taxes			$ 208.33	$ 2,500.00			
Travel Fees							
Payroll Salaries			$ 5,000.00	$ 60,000.00			
Blacksmith/Farrier	$ 2,500.00	$ 30,000.00					
	$ 15,000.00	$ 179,500.00	$ 18,758.33	$ 235,100.00	$ 680,000.00	$ 33,758.33	$ 414,

*Annual Expense Figures are an estimate and are subject to change
Financial data represents a 50 Acre horse farm with 25 working employees
and 6 horses

Expenses / Annual Variable

Expenses	Annual Variable
Gas Utilities	$ 2,400.00
Electric	$ 12,000.00
Mortgage	
Phone	
Cable	
Internet	
Entertainment Food	$ 15,000.00
Marketing/Advertising	$ 21,000.00
Funding Manager	
Cleaning Supplies	$ 3,000.00
Vitamins	$ 1,300.00
Purchase land	
Construct buildings	
Repair Premises	
Fence in Land	
Purchase Equipment	
Purchase Electronics	
Purchase Office Supplies	
Gas for company vehicles	$ 4,800.00
Purchase Horses	
Purchase Dogs	
Purchase other animals	
Pet supplies, horse feed/hay	$ 30,000.00
Purchase company vehicles	
Veterinarian Services	$ 30,000.00
Medical	$ 30,000.00
Insurances	
Property Taxes	
Travel Fees	
Payroll Salaries	
Blacksmith/Farrier	$ 30,000.00
	$ 179,500.00

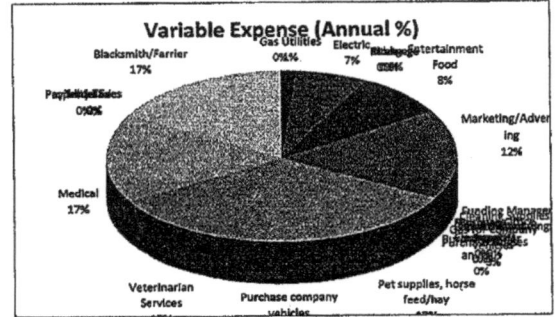

Expenses / Annual Fixed

Expenses	Annual Fixed
Gas Utilities	
Electric	
Mortgage	$ 15,000.00
Phone	$ 1,200.00
Cable	$ 1,200.00
Internet	$ 1,200.00
Entertainment Food	
Marketing/Advertising	
Funding Manager	$ 144,000.00
Cleaning Supplies	
Vitamins	
Purchase land	
Construct buildings	
Repair Premises	
Fence in Land	
Purchase Equipment	
Purchase Electronics	
Purchase Office Supplies	
Gas for company vehicles	
Purchase Horses	
Purchase Dogs	
Purchase other animals	
Pet supplies, horse feed/hay	
Purchase company vehicles	
Veterinarian Services	
Medical	
Insurances	$ 10,000.00
Property Taxes	$ 2,500.00
Travel Fees	
Payroll Salaries	$ 60,000.00
Blacksmith/Farrier	
	$ 235,100.00

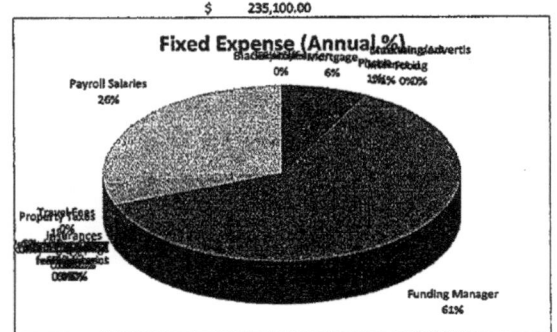

Expenses / Initial Startup

Expenses	Startup
Gas Utilities	
Electric	
Mortgage	
Phone	
Cable	
Internet	
Entertainment Food	
Marketing/Advertising	
Funding Manager	
Cleaning Supplies	
Vitamins	
Purchase land	$ 150,000.00
Construct buildings	$ 150,000.00
Repair Premises	$ 50,000.00
Fence in Land	$ 25,000.00
Purchase Equipment	$ 200,000.00
Purchase Electronics	$ 50,000.00
Purchase Office Supplies	$ 10,000.00
Gas for company vehicles	
Purchase Horses	$ 5,000.00
Purchase Dogs	$ 5,000.00
Purchase other animals	$ 5,000.00
Pet supplies, horse feed/hay	
Purchase company vehicles	$ 30,000.00
Veterinarian Services	
Medical	
Insurances	
Property Taxes	
Travel Fees	
Payroll Salaries	
Blacksmith/Farrier	
	$ 680,000.00

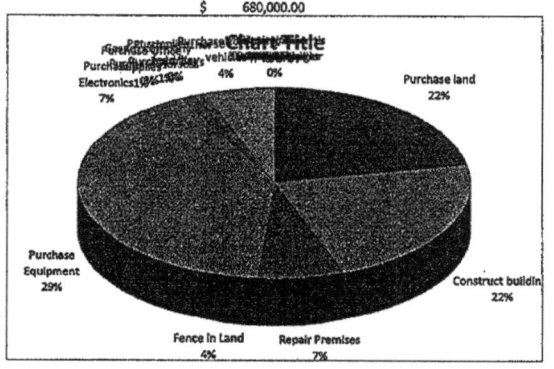

VA's Supportive Services for Veteran Families Program
Exhibit III: Applicant Budget - Quarterly SSVF Grant Funds Budget
*Please note that the SSVF application instructions for Exhibit III refer to monthly expenditure projections. Applicants need only project quarterly expenditures in this submission.

Name of Applicant:	Animal Rescue & Veteran Support Services, Corp.
	DBA Veteran Rescue
SSVF Grant Amount:	$1,000,000.00
Application Fiscal Year:	FY 2013

Program Expenses			% of Total SSVF Grant	SSVF Grant Funds Total Annual	SSVF Grant Funds Quarter 1	SSVF Grant Funds Quarter 2	SSVF Grant Funds Quarter 3	SSVF Grant Funds Quarter 4
1. Provision and Coordination of Supportive Services (Minimum of 90% of Total SSVF Grant Amount)								
1. Personnel/Labor	F FTE	% FTE	Base Annual Salary/Wage					
Title and Organization								
President Veteran Rescue			50,000.00	6%	$2,145.00	13,000.00	13,000.00	15,300.00	13,585.00
Executive Assistant Veteran Rescue				3%	28,385.00	7,000.00	7,000.00	7,000.00	7,000.00
Veteran Veteran Rescue				3%	99,900.00	7,000.00	7,000.00	7,000.00	7,000.00
Ranch Hands Veteran Rescue				3%	28,800.00	3,600.00	7,500.00	7,500.00	7,500.00
Rehabilitation Therapist Veteran Rescue			18%	210,000.00	45,000.00	50,000.00	61,000.00	51,970.00
Interns Veteran Rescue				3%	24,000.00	8,000.00	1,300.00	5,000.00	5,000.00
Medical Staff Veteran Rescue				20%	200,000.00	50,000.00	53,000.00	53,000.00	50,000.00
Cleaning Staff Veteran Rescue				10%	45,600.00	10,000.00	13,000.00	10,000.00	3,600.00
				0%					
				0%					
				0%	-	-	-	-	-
				0%					
				0%	-	-	-	-	-
				0%	-	-	-	-	-
				0%	-	-	-	-	-
				0%					
				3%					
Subtotal Salaries/Wages				34%	308,349.00	135,090.00	135,600.00	345,600.00	154,245.00
Fringe Benefits 0				3%					
Subtotal Personnel				34%	308,349.00	158,800.00	135,000.00	148,400.00	154,345.00
2. Temporary Financial Assistance				0.00%					
3. Other Non-Personnel Provision and Coordination of Supportive Services Expenses								
Required VA Training Development				0%	2,000.00				
Hotel/GAP Training				0%	2,000.00	2,000.00			
Purchase of Facilities				30%	300,000.00	280,000.00	10,000.00	190,000.00	50,000.00
Therapeutic Board				1%	10,000.00	5,000.00	5,000.00		
Supplies				2%	20,100.00	6,100.00	5,000.00	3,000.00	1,300.00
				0%					
				0%					
				0%					
				0%					
				0%	-	-	-	-	-
				0%					
				0%	-	-	-	-	-
				0%					
				0%					
				3%					
				3%					
				3%					
Subtotal Other Program Expenses				34%	895,100.00	125,100.00	80,000.00	193,000.00	51,000.00
5. Lease & Maintenance of Vehicle(s)	# of Vehicles 1			4%	18,000.00	4,000.00	4,500.00	4,000.00	4,500.00
Subtotal Provision and Coordination of Supportive Services				91.04%	905,449.00	278,100.00	309,000.00	258,700.00	169,348.00
2. Administrative Expenses (Maximum of 10% of Total SSVF Grant Amount)								
General Liability Insurance				3%	370.00				370.00
Directors and Officers Insurance				2%	694.00	694.00			
Health Insurance				1%	6,000.00	1,500.00	1,500.00	1,500.00	1,500.00
Administrator Director Fitzcrhd				4%	70,000.00	10,000.00	20,000.00	18,000.00	18,000.00
Travel Expenses				0%	1,000.00	100.00	100.00	100.00	
Utilities				0%	2,847.00	948.00	948.00	948.00	
Office Equipment				0%	4,000.00	1,000.00	1,000.00	1,000.00	1,000.00
				0%					
				0%					
				0%					
				0%					
				0%					
				0%					
				0%					
				0%	-	-	-	-	-
				0%					
Subtotal Administrative Expenses				8.06%	90,551.00	28,683.00	23,049.00	18,949.00	18,070.00
Grand Total			100.00%	1,000,000.00	307,683.00	216,949.00	273,949.00	198,419.00
% of Total SSVF Grant				100.0%	30.8%	21.7%	27.4%	19.8%

Veteran Rescue 2014 Budget

Expense Type	Amount	Repeat Payment?	Notes
Endicia Shipping Postage	$180.00	See notes	$15 monthly
Homes for Heroes vids	$1,000.00	Daily	
Office space rental (TN)	$0.00	See notes	$120/mo when afford
Kentucky alliance domain	$0.00	See notes	Shiela Clover English
Trademark Press	$1,600.00	No	
Credit card payment	$0.00	No	Reimburse for this when afford
Brighthouse PSA	$5,200.00	No	$100 a spot per VP
Corp. vehicle	$5,000.00	No	Used value
Home repair projects	$1,000.00	No	8A Certification needed
Purchase ranch (TN)	$0.00	See notes	$50,000 for 50 acres w/home
Purchase Ranch VA	$250,000.00	No	
Pet supplies	$20,000.00	No	covers dogs cats horses bunnies etc
Property taxes	$5,000.00	Yearly	
Gen liability insurance/D&O Ins	$2,000.00	No	
Legal Counsel Retainer	$0.00	No	
Car Insurance	$1,524.00	See notes	$127 monthly
Path certification	$800.00	No	Per person
First aid certification	$65.00	No	Per person
Health/dental/vision insurance	$18,176.40	Yearly	For 4 people, $1514.70/mo
Marketing	$0.00	See notes	Budget for FY 2015
Travel	$1,000.00	No	
Car repairs	$0.00	No	engine shipping/fluids paid
Laptop	$0.00	See notes	paid off
File Retrieval from Hard Drive	$400.00	No	Seagate
Video conference software	$0.00	See notes	$50 month Ask Jack to recommend one
Salaries	$100,000.00	No	when Veteran Rescue can afford performance bas
Bank Fees	$0.00	No	paid off
Past due corp bills	$0.00	No	paid w/July CFC
Duns & Bradstreet	$0.00	See notes	Price per company. $500 estimate based on sale
Office supplies	$1,500.00	No	8A Certification needed
Signage	$0.00		paid off
Financial Mgmt	$0.00	See notes	$1500 yr only when we have over $25000 invest
Total Expenses	**$414,445.40**		

Income Type	Amount	Repeat Payment?	Notes
CFC	$9,451.52	See Notes	April: 190.91, July: 3086.87, October: 3086.87, March 2015: 3086.87
CFC AI	$209.86	No	
Paypal Donations	$300.00	See Notes	$25 monthly minus fees
Donation tables	$1,500.00	See Notes	June-August; 500 each
Coffee cup sales	$3,300.00	No	July 4th event
Wildcat's Sanctuary & Ranch donation	$3,500.00	See Notes	Payment depends on Wildcat income
(Wildcat) Stock	$0.00	See Notes	$250 each, 5000 available
TTWC	$2,500.00	See Notes	December: also donates pet supplies
TTWC Fundraiser	$5,000.00	See Notes	Dog O Ween
Grants	$10,000.00	See Notes	200 submitted, money granted TBA
Fred Sale of Veteran Rescue Items	$750.00		Cups, Paracord, Shirts, etc. signs and banner
Auction	$500.00	see Notes	Min open bid Portraits
Trey Annual donation	$500.00		
Benefactor/Sponsor Donations	$5,000.00		Fundraising Event Money and Benefactor annual donation

grant responses

September 18, 2014. The Summerlee Foundation $5000
- Shumaker Foundation declined
- Patterson foundation declined
- Quail Roost Foundation, no funding yet. Keep us in mind.
- Emily Vernon Foundation Followed up 4/23/14
- NAVS asked us to reapply using different terminology.
- Binky Foundation Declined
- Scaife Family Foundation declined
- Maddie Fund declined
- Amaturo Family Foundation declined
- Park Foundation declined
- Robert J. Kleberg, Jr. and Helen C. Kleberg Foundation Declined
- The Charter Foundation November Board meeting
- The Kettering Family Foundation online where trustees reside Nov
- B.H. Breslauer Foundation Inc Declined
- William G Selby and Marie Selby Foundation Declined 3 county
- Dorothea Haus Ross Foundation Declined

	Amount	
Total Income	$42,511.38	
Net Income	-$371,934.02	

CFC Reponses
- UNIVERSAL GIVING NOW OPEN CFC # 19270
- Central Fl approved
- Atlantic Coast denied
- Ft Campbell Approved
- TN/KY Approved
- Suncoast approved
- NE Fl/SE GA approved

grant responses
- At least 70 applications outstanding as of 07/04/14
- The AWC Family Foundation Board meet this Summer
- Resources Legacy Fund Declined
- Americana Foundation Declined
- Access Fund Declined

Where To Go For Funding

Angel Investors, Venture capitalists, Bank, Friends and Family, Sale of Stock, Donations, Contracts, etc. Let's take each of these one at a time to see what might be right for you.

First off your personal credit score has a lot to do with how your approval or denial comes about. Your Business Plan is next to get dissected. Marketing Plan and your personal enthusiasm as you present your 60 second elevator speech also make an impact.

Be careful where you find these sources, as there are a ton of scammers out there including on LinkedIn.

Angels: I can vouch for three out of hundreds I've approached. Do your homework. Find a reputable agency or person who can vouch for one.

Venture Capital: Again I met hundreds through LinkedIn and Google Searches. Only one was legit.

Bank: Must have a very high personal credit score, 10% of funds you are asking for minimum, and equity in home too. That will get you a maybe. Some banks restrict where you can apply for a mortgage or a line of credit. Bank loans too vary. I've dealt with at least six different banks both local and national.

Friends and Family: Unless they are a millionaire with money to burn, don't ask. Unless you like being lonely and shunned, don't ask.

Stock: Corporations can have shares of stock issued and can sell personally to known associates and family to avoid any SEC rulings and fines. Small and startups go this route. But stock is worthless practically speaking until after three years in business making a profit.

Donations: Not For Profits go this route. This includes the CFC Program (Combined Federal Contribution). 100% Tax Deductible. This is how 99% of non-profits operate and survive from year to year.

Contracts: Levy Restaurants will contract with your nonprofit organization to donate to your cause. You work for your money. We started out doing this until there was a management change which altered the rules of size of organizations that could work.

Government Contracts are the biggie every for profit wants: Millions of dollars per year. The process for this is long, time consuming, and then you bid, and then you also have to be on the GSA Schedule or Categories to get noticed. Don't bother paying the companies that call you up unless you have money to burn. Find someone already working on contract and get their help if possible. Otherwise if left with no choice pay $300/year.

Thinking Outside The Box

How many of you entrepreneurs think outside the box when it comes to getting clients or raising funds? I learned that after three years of networking my companies I had to do something different if I wanted my companies to thrive.

So for my nonprofit since traditional fundraising methods didn't work for my situation, it was time for outside the box solutions. Golf tournaments are nice and all but if you can't get more than 16 people to sign up in 9 months it's time to go elsewhere, which I did.

Alas the same goes for a for profit company. Since banks, investors, friends, and family are all out the door for solutions to generating start up capitol, I have moved onto ...wait for it...writing a book and self-publishing to bring in revenue. Having worked as an Assistant Manager and Bookseller in the book world I know the ins/outs there pretty well. Barnes and Noble in my opinion is struggling, Borders which owned Waldenbooks went under, actually I think Barnes and Nobles bought them out too. Wholesale discount bargain books went under. Amazon and Kindle and small bookstores are pretty much where you go to sell. Plus by using Smile.Amazon.com to purchase (Amazon's donation site exact same as Amazon.com) you're helping your nonprofit generate donations by purchasing.

Using my knowledge, and my style of writing and knowing where to go to get things done means anyone can do this. There are literally hundreds of business books most of which I found wordy and of no help at all,-even those with big names in the business world.

By writing a business book that is specific for small businesses, is short and to the point, it is immediately useful to all, and by self-publishing it is immediately available to all for sale on Amazon or Kindle.

I do a lot of networking and collaborating to help others. I don't charge for this as people say I should. I collaborate with other small startup nonprofits mostly because they need the help and I've already been there.

If you have a non for profit that is a 501c3 approved, then you can also speak to executives at local airports asking if they will donate space so your organization can sell your products to everyone passing through. In my case coffee cups or   T-Shirts or Paracord Items, etc. You get the idea.

Donation Table Events outside your local stores. You contact the Store Manager for assistance in getting on their calendar.

Standing in the Medians at Stop lights with a donation container. You see the City Tax Collector Office for that one.

So when you decide you want to start a business, no matter the type, start thinking and planning years in advance for budgeting matters. If traditional fundraising doesn't work for you, or you just bootstrap it, go to thinking outside the box. In the business world it does not matter if what you try comes from an era bygone, if it works go with it. Don't just try one avenue, try them all until you find what works, then tweak it as needed.

#Christihubbard #business #book #fundraise #forprofit #nonprofit

Let Me Know Your Thoughts

Wildcat's Sanctuary and Ranch clients all received coffee cups from Veteran Rescue as appreciation gifts. All of our Event Sponsors received Veteran Rescue Coffee Cups as Appreciation gifts and two received T-Shirts and Polo Shirts that said Veteran Rescue on them.

Veteran Rescue Feedback Poll

Animal Rescue & Veteran Support Services Trade name Veteran Rescue is looking for feedback.

Who liked receiving appreciation gifts from us?
Raffle gifts?
What types of gifts did you like best out of what we offered?
Where could we improve?

Who likes seeing all the updates we do when we have a fundraiser going on?

Do you like seeing real time updates, before and after results?

Let us know what you think!

Animal Rescue & Veteran Support Services Trade name Veteran Rescue

Wildcat's Sanctuary and Ranch Corp

I have added both businesses to Angie's List. Review links are as follows: http://angieslist.com/review/8332752 Link to write a review for Veteran Rescue

http://angieslist.com/review/8332744 Link to write a review for Wildcat's Sanctuary and Ranch

Honesty, Integrity, Ethics, Accountability

You make or break your business reputation with each contact you make. With each program you offer, with each person you help. You must have honor, integrity, and ethics or you will be shut down by the IRS or State Officials. Ever wonder why your business has slowed to nothing? Why all your emails come back as spam? Let's think about how long you have been in business. Is your reputation torn to shreds over perceived slights?

Make sure the timeline you give for any event or project is realistic. Always communicate to the other party involved if anything changes. Minimum time for any fundraising is six weeks for raffles and auctions to nine months for golf tournaments and black tie dinners.

Accountability. Is it just for audits?

What does accountability mean to you? To your business? Is it just for audits? I sure hope not.

As you know I have three different types of companies and I have controls for all three that works for me. It ensures I have accountability at all times and cruise through any audits that come up for various reasons.

This control works when applying for grants, when applying for CFC, when the IRS asks for information, when a potential donor requests to see documentation, when asking for a bank loan, a line of credit, etc. You get the idea.

I love it when funds are "guaranteed" only to arrive late or not at all. Just how many excuses can one person come up with to excuse this? Do you think your vendors or clients care about them? The answer is NO. It really is a balancing act when dealing with vendors, clients, and other organizations.

If someone on your Advisory Board tells you point blank not to collect documentation of any kind, it's time to set them straight or ask them to leave. If they say one thing and then do another, it's time to go. That's a version of fraud when it comes to funds for your charity. They ask you to add a program that falls within your Mission and then turns out to be a "slush fund" that you were not informed of, it's time to hold a meeting to let everyone know what's going on. The fact that the perpetrator is a Veteran owned business that partnered with you is just one reason why they're getting such a bad reputation.

Another situation that came up was a Veteran with PTSD/TBI made worse with drug problems and memory issues. The VA had him on over a dozen different medicines. He started appointing people to my board with no authority. He then wanted 100% of funds that came into the program he was in charge of for himself, not the program. The Board voted him off after he was apprised of the laws he was breaking and fraud he was perpetrating.

A Veteran wanted to partner with Veteran Rescue on a handshake deal, no legal documents signed of any kind. Again he had PTSD/Medication. Did not happen.

PTSD was just one of the things they had in common. I'm pretty sure they all lacked jobs, or were really tight for funding. I tried to find Board Members who had skills I lacked. I have multiple programs that help Veterans and animals nationwide. I focus on Florida for the animals, and do what I can for the rest.

People will try to take advantage of you especially if you're a woman owned company. You need people who support you not take you for every penny they can. If anything, they should respect my organization's transparency and commitment to have an above board and top running operation.

Sample of Recent Not For Profit Board Meeting issues:

I do have non-disclosure forms to be signed and returned. I believe maybe we should be enforcing that rule for our Board.

My organization is an open book. Receipts are on file, client files are confidential, and my 990 is in full public view on my website, Charity Navigator and more.

To question my honesty and integrity and then say you didn't mean to offend but then to say don't make me your enemy I will sabotage you publicly is an offense.

You can see I have been helping others including Veterans as much as I possibly can given financial resources we have. It has not been two years between helping Veterans.

Yes Veteran Rescue has accumulated expenses that do need to be paid.

Yes it is legal to use your personal vehicle for business purposes and write off the repairs, mileage, gas, and more.

The organization is healthier than ever this year.

Yes it is legal to ask for documentation such as DD214, medical diagnosis, military ID, estimates from contractors and more including photos of before and after repairs for clients requesting assistance. Every nonprofit, government agency, VA, etc. asks for it before treating. It is required for audits among other reasons. It is kept confidential. Not one of my clients have complained.

This keeps are budget reasonable and our clients legit. We do not have bottomless pockets to help every person who says I tell the truth. We have learned our lessons there over the years.

Sample of Recent Board Agenda including event calendar dates: Current budget numbers updated, see attached Excel.

Fundraisers: CFC, TTWC, Donation Table, Removed for privacy Raffle, Auction, coffee cups. What did we learn? Are there any changes we should implement?

Bills: Past due all paid off but two.

Moving Forward. Purchasing Ranch, Travel, Marketing, Video, Programs

This will be the first year we will have a surplus of funds. They must be utilized wisely in case of emergencies.

Refresher on Veteran Rescue for our Board Members in other states who will be representing us and speaking with CFC employees. VA Hospitals, Post Offices, Military Bases, etc.

Who we are, what we do, how we help, why we help. Documentation we collect on clients and why we do, Documentation we need for audits.

Sample of Recent Results of this kind of meeting: New meeting features: Skype call recorder! This is to help Melissa dictate notes, or for anything we may have to refer back to at a later date, etc. If you have a problem with being recorded, please let us know before the meeting!

Voting:

1. Add a program (Sponsor MMA Training for Veterans with PTSD with proper documentation) if yes TN only or Nationwide? Cap of how many a year?

Against having no documentation [everyone except one]

Add a program [no]

Note: Documentation is needed for Veteran Rescue's protection in an audit. Per Removed for privacy – there is a stigma with documentation, insults PTSD Veterans and are looking forward to more of a "handshake" deal

2. Change how we do fundraisers, types of fundraisers, length of time we hold one, who we allow to host on our behalf, etc.

Six weeks minimum timeframe is required in order to host a fundraiser for Veteran Rescue. All funds agreed upon up front must remain and cannot be changed without mutual agreement by both parties.

Anyone in possession of Veteran Rescue, signage, banners, products, etc, must pay up front costs associated with them so Veteran Rescue programs can continue without interruption.

Removed for privacy: $750

3. Cap or tweak our current programs. If yes, what do we do about our waiting list?

Removed for privacy - Limited amount of services, don't spread yourself too thin. Can be fluid, based on donations

Voted to keep current programs on website. Home repair project is being capped and may not be continued after finishing the current waiting list

4. Prune our Board Members down as recommended? Change how we pick them, where we pick them from, serve with no voting rights for a specific term until voted in or out?

Pruning: Removed for privacy – yes [7]. We appreciate your service and abilities on our behalf, including the fundraising raffle. We wish you the best of luck in your future endeavors. Your support is more than welcome in any future events.

Future Board Members will be added by a vote after serving several months as an intern to see if they are a good fit. Non-disclosure Document signed up front.

5. Partnerships/Collaborations with other entities: Yes/No/With limits (what documentation would we require)

Within limits – the board must vote and documentation and a non-disclosure agreement is required up front.

Veteran organization provided collaboration document written by an attorney, was passed by the board as sufficient MMA gym documentation is required for a collaboration, however the sponsor a veteran with PTSD for MMA training will not be a part of the programs we offer.

Thank you all for going out of your way to assist us.

Veteran Rescue is participating in several CFC Events where we have a table and we speak to others. August Events. Others will be added as they are offered.

Oct 26, 1-4PM Temple Terrace Womans Club Fundraiser, FL

Nov 2nd, Board Meeting 1PM EST: 2 grants being decided on for Veteran Rescue

Dec 7th, 1PM EST Board Meeting

*********UNIVERSAL GIVING APPROVED BEGINNING THIS YEAR, ANYONE WHO HAS OUR CFC #19270, CAN GIVE MONEY TO US REGARDLESS OF LOCATION!!***************

Please come see us at these events or ask us to come speak at your events.

Winning Awards and Marketing

I have to date six awards for the last four years for two of my companies combined. This has brought me business to my door when I published that information on my websites, and on all forms of social media. I have videos, photos, and dozens of referrals I put on my website from others who have sent me the referral.

My Marketing plan actually came to me as a gift from Nova University School of Business Students of Professor Dena Hale. I can't thank her enough.

I have two different types of business plans. One is 8 right pages, KISS Method, and the bank loved it. The other has the Marketing Plan for Nova University in it and the banks raved as did the investors. This business plan is over 30 pages long. It has the same outline as the first but is not using KISS Method.

I don't know the first thing about Marketing, so I utilize my family that excel in I.T. My webmaster is WordPress Happy which uses plugins that do the bulk of my marketing for me and it's free.

Another form of marketing is having a space donated for your use and putting up a donation table, selling items for charity, Advertising on Billboard signs and paying for commercial spots on TV and radio.

PSA's or Public Service Announcements. When any nonprofit are offered these, go for them! They are free to the organization and bring in tons of new supporters and donations. Once you have a PSA in hand upload that video to all your websites, all your social media sites, upload to YouTube, and pop into emails to friends and family to share.

Websites: Do It Yourself and Look Great

WordPress is my friend and yours. Easy to use, free, and deals with the ugly side of Marketing and SEO Optimization, etc. Your Website looks and feels professional, and I can update it myself without needing a computer tech's help.

There is absolutely no need to pay thousands of dollars for this service. Believe me, unless you have money to burn, just ignore all those sales emails and phone calls.

Domains:

Who needs to pay $30 when $5 or $9 will do? I purchased my domains through Cheap Domain and some were on sale through Web or Register. Both of those sites though will scam you for thousands of dollars and as such I don't use them for anything other than my on sale domain name.

BlueHost is who I have my paid web hosting through. Easy to use, very helpful when you call, and did not cost me an arm and a leg. I am able to have all my businesses hosted for free on this server and all my other business domains are also hosted for free plus unlimited emails, etc.

As of this writing I have 20 domains on my server with multiple emails for each one and all of it looks professional.

If you want to go professional instead of do it yourself I recommend Computer Tech's Castle. http://computertechscastle.com/ Affordable, reliable, quick service by qualified personnel.

Halogix Technologies

Social Media Is your Friend

LinkedIn, Facebook, Twitter, and YouTube just to name a few of the big ones you will want to create accounts for. It is important that each business, each personal account be kept separate. For instance I have three businesses and a personal account with each. I also ~~of~~ have separate groups for my businesses on LinkedIn.

This is a great way to build your brand and your reputation. By posting every day at least three times a day at different hours you will see an increase in traffic to your website and office.

LinkedIn is where I receive 90% of my business referrals and supporters worldwide. It is also how I contacted local radio stations, newspapers, celebrities, and business owners we could utilize resources from.

Local radio stations and online radio such as Readers Entertainment and Chairborne Commandos and SOFREP are all good sources of online radio publicity spots for not for profits. This in turn drives website traffic and donations as well as offers for volunteering, other agencies or organizations looking to do a community project, etc.

Some radio stations are owned by one big corporation and will typically repeat or re-air your interview without it looking like a repeat interview at different times or month or quarter. For instance Clear Channel Radio owns over 80 stations nationwide so my one interview went nationwide multiple times.

Move on to your local newspapers, reporters, and TV anchors. When you have sufficient notice go to national TV anchors, reporters, and TV Stations airing PSA or interviewing your organization. Each of these events drives web traffic, volunteer offers, and donations of money or in kind.

Make short 1 or 2 minute videos of each project or program. Get client referrals or thank you's and add them to all your sites. Take lots of pictures. Get legal and liability release forms signed so you can use the photos and videos of clients and others you've helped.

We Thank Our Sponsors For Supporting Us!

 Home Makeover Systems is owned by AL Moses.

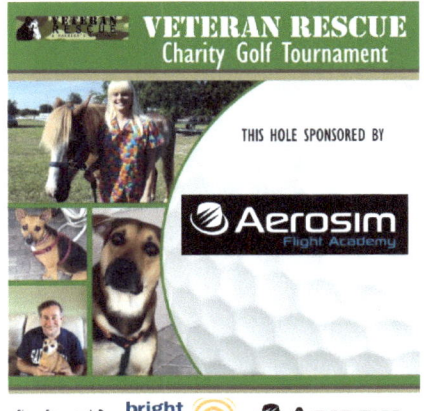 Aerosim VP is Hank Coates.

 **Wildcat's Sanctuary and Ranch, Corp is owned by Christi Hubbard**

 **Trustco Bank VP is Erik Schreck**

Bright House contact Cassandra Whipple

Contact Elaine Coniglio

Veteran Rescue owner is

Christi Hubbard

THE END